LONG, TALL, SHORT AND HAIRY POEMS

Sam McBratney is the well-loved author of many children's books, including the favourite *Guess How Much I Love You*. An ex-teacher, he has also written stories and radio plays for adults, and is the winner of several literary prizes. *Long, Tall, Short and Hairy Poems* is his first poetry collection. Married, with three grown-up children, Sam McBratney lives in County Antrim, Northern Ireland.

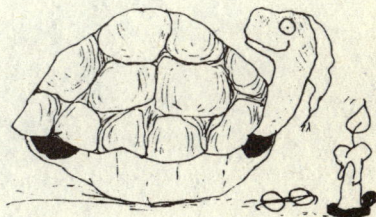

Long
TALL
SHORT and
~~HAIRY~~
POEMS

by
Sam McBratney

illustrated by Stephen Lewis

h
Hodder
Children's
Books

a division of Hodder Headline plc

A Catalogue record for this book is
available from the British Library

ISBN 0340 66494 0

Hodder Children's Books
A division of Hodder Headline plc
338 Euston Road
London NW1 3BH

Printed and bound in Great Britain
by The Guernsey Press Co. Ltd, Guernsey, Channel Islands

Contents

Off to Africa!

On the wire they gather
in a nearly-ready row,

They won't shiver in the winter
when the cold winds blow.

I wonder: which wee swallow
has the job of shouting GO!

Meece

If mouses are mice,
   and gooses are geese,
What excuses have mooses
   for not being meece?

Advice about Kangaroos

Now listen, dear.
You must have nothing to do
With a kangaroo.

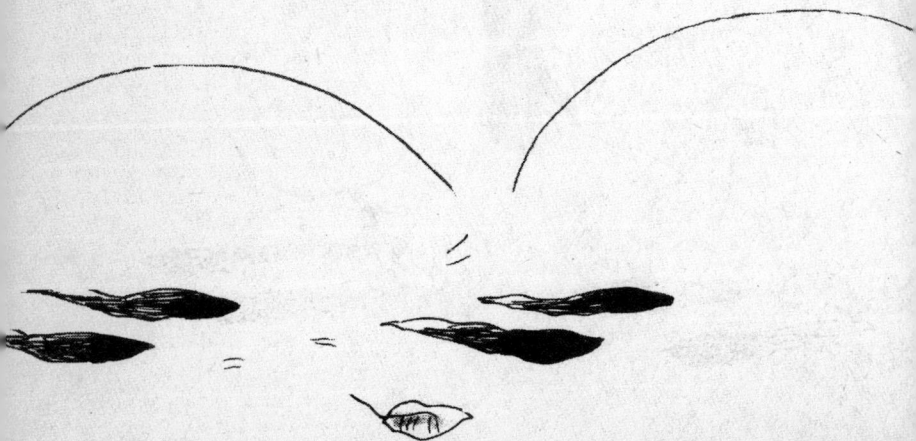

When you're talking to a kangaroo,
   half time he's just not there.
After a word of conversation,
   he shoots into the air!

It's like walking with a yo-yo
   when you're with a kangaroo.
He boings along on feet like skis,
   and expects *you* to do it, too!

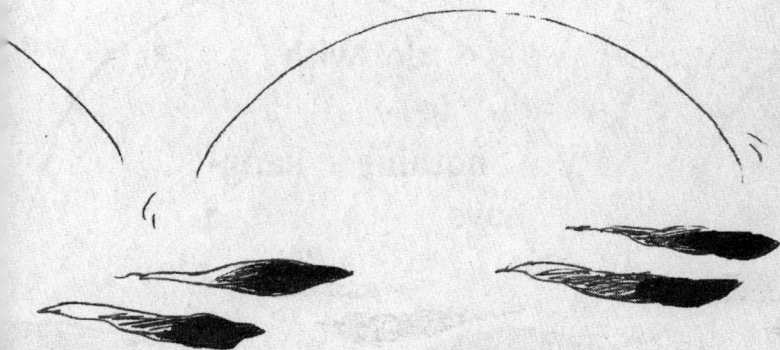

do with
to   a
nothing   kang-
have   a-
So   roo,

thing   N
awful about   I
truly   them   R
the   is   P
for   their S

The one truly awful
thing about them
is their SPRING**G**

Aliens

When you look up on a clear night,
Do you think of time and stars?
Do you wonder if something
    rather strange
Is alive and well on Mars?

Near one of those distant,
    twinkling suns,
Or beyond, in the deep of space,
Is an unknown creature opening
    an eye
In what is – perhaps – a face?

And is there an island in the universe
Where astronauts shall land,
Where the print of a giant foot
    lies waiting
In the interstellar sand?

But wherever starships may go –
What could they find
To boggle the mind more,
Than Earth's own vanished alien,
  the Dinosaur?

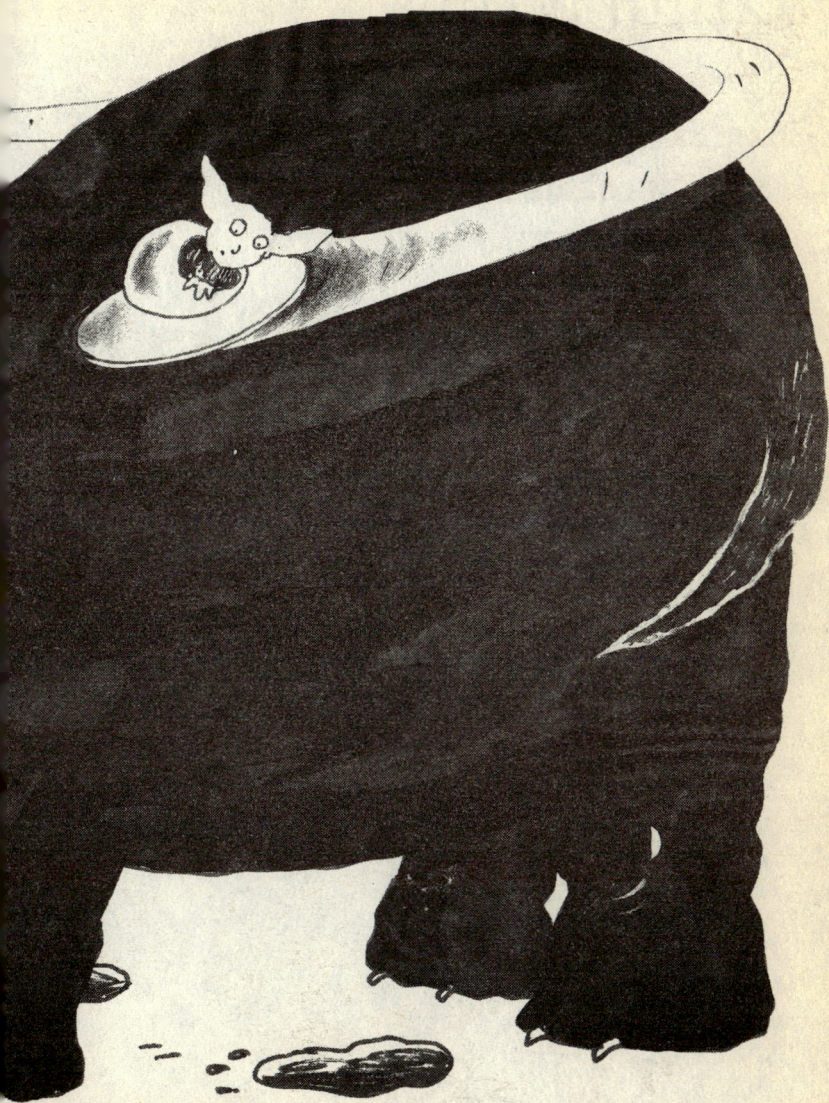

Guillemots

Did you know that guillemots
Are very good at join-the-dots?

Fractions

How much of a giraffe
Is neck?
I've heard
Some say a third.
It might be hard to check,
But I'd say
At least one half
Of a giraffe
Is neck.

Dance, Daddy-long-legs

I saw a daddy-long-legs
    dancing in the rain;
He danced with many friends of his
    across our window pane.

Dance, daddy-long-legs,
    is there anyone who knows
How you can move so easily
    on skinny legs like those?

The Lollipop Toad

How does a frog get over the road?
Do you think he knows his Green
    Cross Code?
When he hops from here to there,
The cars must give him an awful scare.

Maybe he knows
Of secret holes,
Or long, dark tunnels
Dug by moles.

How *does* a frog get over the road?
I think there must be a Lollipop Toad.

The Emu and the Ostrich

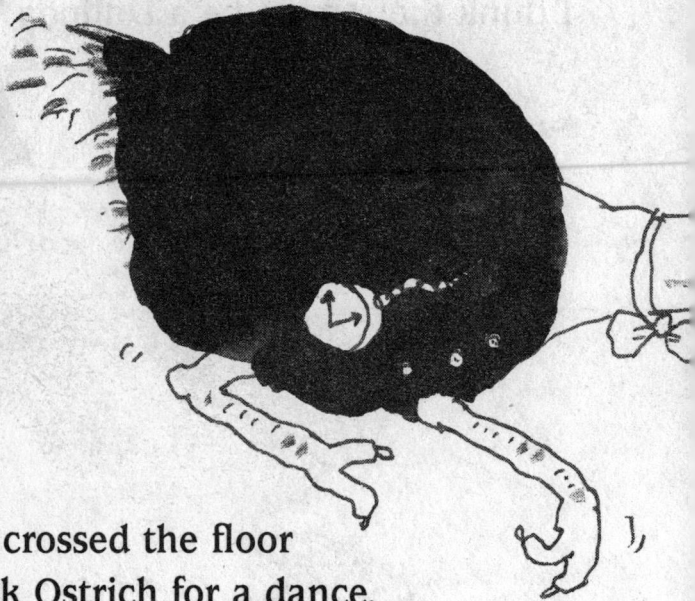

Emu crossed the floor
To ask Ostrich for a dance.
He was looking for adventure
And excitement and romance.

Ostrich saw him coming
And stuck her head beneath her wing;
It was absolutely dark in there,
So she couldn't see a thing.

'The moon is out,' said Emu,
'And I find you very kissable.'
'Go away,' said Ostrich,
'Can't you see that I'm invisible?'

How do you tell?

When I see a hippopotamus,
  I always wonder this:
Is that a hippopotamister,
  or a hippopotamiss?

Daydream

In school today
my mind took me
To see a city
beneath the sea.

The creatures there
had sea-weed hair,
They all saw me
but didn't care.

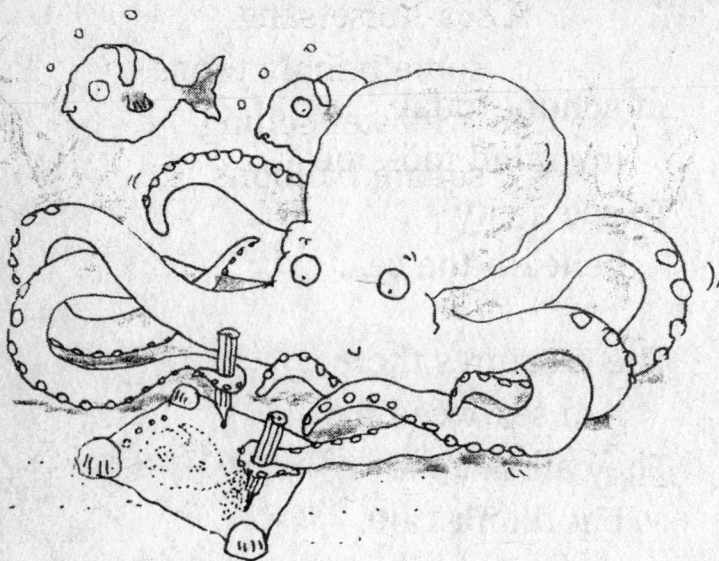

An octopus
   with arms in knots
Patiently
   played join-the-dots.

A sea-horse sang
   some bubbly tunes
To a lobster selling
   square balloons.

And I saw ghostly
sunlight fall
On palaces
with sea-shell walls.

Then a loud voice spoke
    a name like mine:
'Once again, Jennifer –
    what's seven times nine?'

All the heads
    that I could see
Turned this way
    to stare at me.

I blinked.
And just in time said, 'Sixty-three!'

Specs

If there's something that no
rhinoceros lacks,
It's a suitable prop for his
bothersome specs.

The Ladybird Word

Ladybird, ladybird,
How has it occurred
That you are known
By the 'ladybird' word?
   You don't look like a lady.
   You're not even a bird.
So why are you known
By the 'ladybird' word?

Bugs!

Let's talk about things that are useful.
Let's talk about things you can't see.
It's time someone wrote a good poem
About invisible life-forms like ME.

Bugs! We're everywhere.
We're in the water and the air.
Indoors, outdoors, underground,
Wherever you look that's where we're
    found.
We're on your hands, we're on your
    brow,
We're on the page you're reading now.

Bugs!
We can make your tummy funny,
Or a thousand noses runny.
We're the ones who cause infections,
We're the reason for injections.
We're the ones who make you mad
By turning good food into bad.

But let me tell you this about us.
Your human race can't do without us.
In fact, you owe us quite a lot.
If we weren't here to make things rot
The piles of stuff you throw away
Would just get bigger every day.
Rubbish mountains there would be
If you didn't have my friends and me.
Apple cores, potato skins,
All the scraps in all your bins -
We break it up, we cause decay:
In time we rot it all away.

You need plants, and plants can't
   grow
Unless we're in the soil below.
We go to work on last year's leaves,
Making food for next year's trees.
Because of all the work we do,
We make life possible for YOU.

So let's talk about things that are
   useful.
Let's talk about things you can't see.
It's time someone wrote a good poem.
About invisible life-forms like ME.

Tango

If you are ever asked to tango
By an elephant,
Say you can't.
You must refuse,
For after all – we *are* gnus.
Just look him in the eye and tell him
    straight:
'I only do the tango with an ungulate.'

An ungulate is a mammal with hoofs.

Territory

A robin from
   the hazel tree
Perched on my spade,
   and looked at me.

When he saw I wouldn't
   fly away,
He opened his beak,
   and seemed to say:

'Scram, beat it, bye-bye –
   shoo!
All this belongs to me –
   not you.'

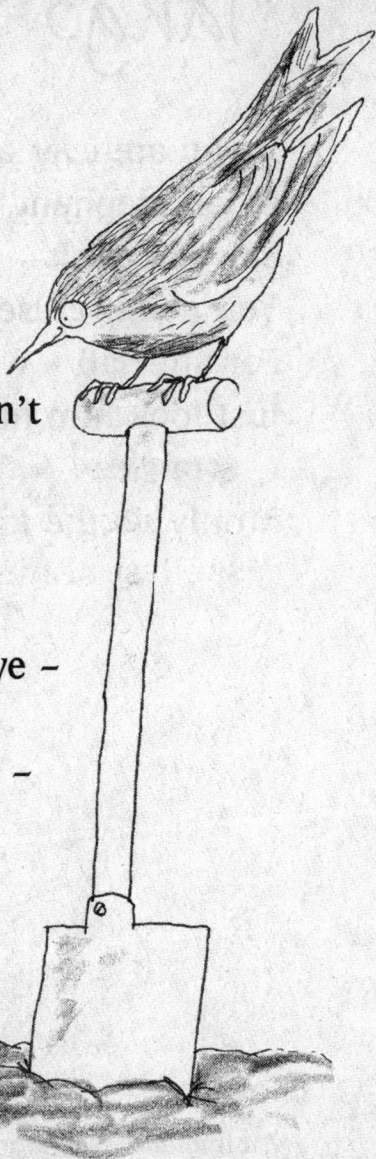

I said, 'Stay or go, bird,
  either is fine.
But this garden isn't yours –
  it's mine.'

He flew away with a
  zoom and a skim,
And I thought I'd seen
  the last of him.

But there he was again today,
    as cheeky and as cross,
'Better not mess with me, Buster,
    I'm the BOSS.'

One hump or two?

No other mammal
has a temper like a camel.

Said Camel One:
    'Two humps are better -
    they're twice as good as one.
    You are obviously unfinished
    and you might as well have *none*!'

Said Camel Two:
    'Rubbish! One single hump per camel
    is the natural amount,
    and it's just too bad, and rather sad,
    that *your* sort cannot count!'

They still don't speak and it's been
   a week
since they first began to fight.
And so it will be until both agree
   that the other one was right.

Is it not amazing
that creatures of such bulk
should feel the need to sulk?

The Ate o'Clock Croc

Once I met a crocodile
With a clock tied to his nose.
   I also saw
    on his back left paw
Ten bells upon his toes.

And around his wrinkled neck were
    hung
Some lovely pink carnations.
    I'm rather shy,
    but I asked him why
He wore these decorations.

The crocodile crept closer,
And winked one bulging eye.
    The clock went tick
    as he seemed to lick
An imaginary pie.

'Well, I'm going to a wedding,
And don't wish to be late.
    Do be a dear,
    come over here,
And tell me if my clock says eight.'

'I see your clock from here,' I said.
'And the time's not hard to tell.
  I can safely state
  that it's almost ate –
And I'm glad that I can spell.'

So I said goodbye to the crocodile
With the clock tied to his nose.
  And he licked his teeth
  as the bells beneath
Tinkled on his back left toes.

The Habits
of Bats

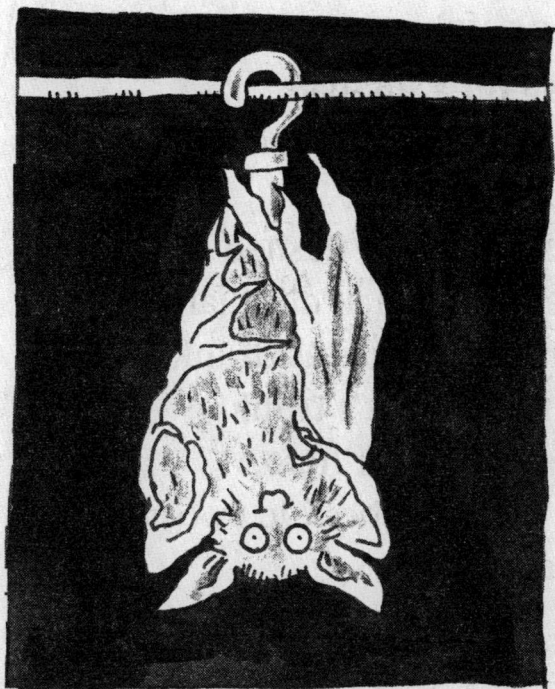

The bats in our barn
   are interesting fellas.
They hang themselves up
   like folded umbrellas.

The Elegant Amphibian

Relaxing on a lily-pad
Lay an elegant amphibian.
His coat was green
And his dark eyes flashed
Like flakes of black obsidian.
   Then his water was drunk
   by an elephant's trunk.
'Oh well,' said our hero,
'I shall wait for the tide to come in
   again.'

What am I?

People do not like me much.
I'm the something in the grass
That makes them quake.
People do not like me much.
They prefer hedgehogs, badgers, birds
And such.
They like animals with soft brown eyes
And cuddly fur,
Especially if they bark or purr.
But me?
I'm the something in the grass
That makes them quake.
Elephants they adore,
Gorillas galore,
Lions that roar,
Even the died-out dinosaur –
And polar bears, chimps, orang-outangs
(These have no poison in their fangs.)

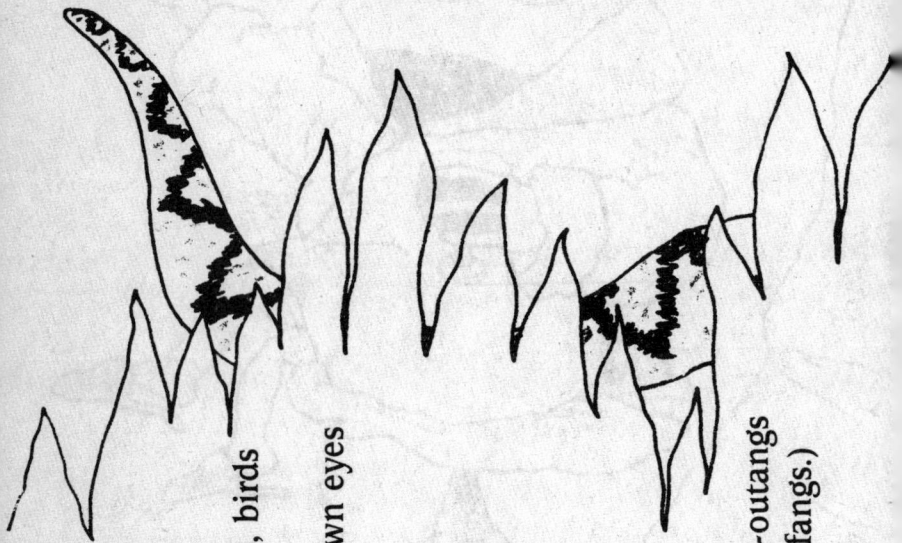

But I'm the one they cannot take ~
The something in the grass
That makes them quake.
I'm a rattler, I'm a battler,
I'm a winder, I'm a binder,
I'm a surreptitious sneaker
And a creeper-up-behind-her.
I'm a glider and a slider,
I'm a curly-wurly slitherer,
A wallower, a swallower,
A biter,
A spitter and a hitter,
And a strike-with-all-my-mighter,
A squeezer sort of geezer
Fond of strangulating seizure.
I'm a hisser not a kisser,
More alarming than I'm charming.
I'm the something in the grass
That rhymes with. . . quake.

The Barnacle Batch

A batch of barnacles sailed the world
  on the back of a blue-nosed whale.
They were well stuck on with
    barnacle glue
    to a spot near the end of the tail.

Now the whale didn't know
that they were there,
so she didn't ask them
to pay a fare.
And the barnacle batch
didn't offer to pay,
for they weren't aware
that they'd been away.

Longevity

The Hare met the Tortoise
At a downtown gig,
And spoke to him, intending to impress:
   'Let's face it, Tortoise –
   you're a mess.
   Man, it's so embarrassing,
   where's your sense of dress?
   The thing about you is,
   you've got no go, there ain't no *fizz*.
   Living in that upturned bowl,
   you just weren't made to rock
   and roll.'

The Tortoise thought this over
In his quiet way,
And allowed his eyes a solitary blink.
   'I'm not much bothered, Hare,
   by what you think.
   I'm not the sort of fool
   who thinks he's cool,
   and it has never been my practice
   to prance about in pink.
   And as for lacking fizz,
   this is not so bad as it appears.
   You'll be gone, and *I'll* be here,
   in another hundred years.'

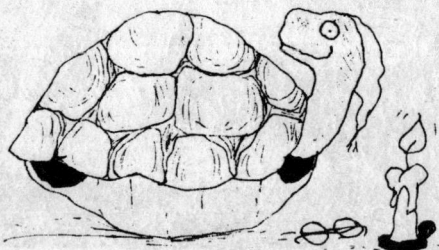

Prisoners

When I was small
As I recall,
We dug holes in the ground.
We marked the graves where
    loved-ones lay
    with buttercups we found.

First of all
When I was small,
I owned an ornamental fish.
This swam in golden circles round
   the prison of its dish.

My heart was set
On a different pet,
So I bought myself a bird.
In loneliness she sometimes spoke
   a solitary word.

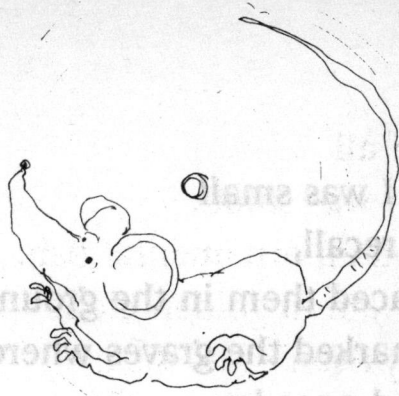

The mouse I had
Was quite a lad –
He ran and ran all day.
Although his wheel went round and
    round,
        he did not run away.

And through the wire
I did admire
My bunny's splendid ears.
The food she ate was mainly green
    throughout her captive years.